STUDIO GHIBLI
THE UNOFFICIAL COOKBOOK

Recipes by Minh-Tri Vo
Photography concocted by Apolline Cartier
Background texts cooked up by Claire-France Thévenon
Translated by Lisa Molle-Troyer

INSIGHT
EDITIONS

SAN RAFAEL · LOS ANGELES · LONDON

IMAGE CREDITS:

CONTENTS

MAIN DISHES

DESSERTS

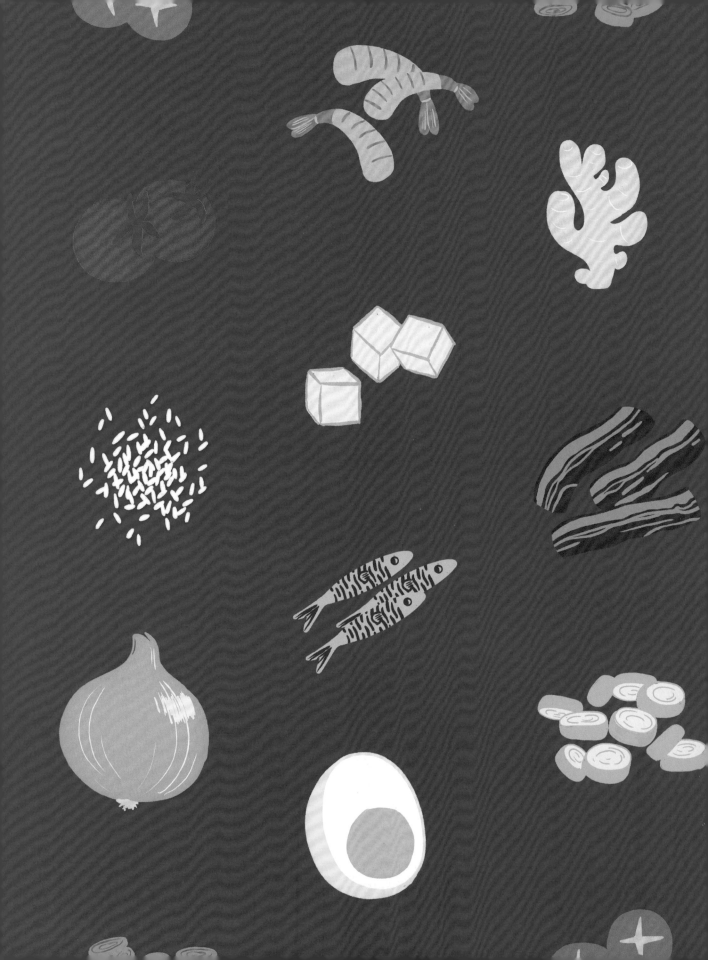

MAIN DISHES

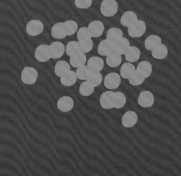

MY NEIGHBOR TOTORO
Hayao Miyazaki, 1988

TOTORO'S BENTO

BACKGROUND

A popular and easy-to-make lunch in Japan, a bento is a packed meal served in a box. Bentos can be bought prepackaged from a *konbini* (twenty-four-hour convenience store) or, more traditionally, made from scratch. These packaged meals reflect the balance we expect from Japanese food, consisting mainly of rice, a serving of protein, and some accompanying fruits or vegetables. Although the basic concept is similar to any packed lunch, calling a bento a "lunch box" overlooks one of its most distinctive features: aesthetics. A bento should *look* as good as it tastes. Beautiful bento boxes are a source of pride for many Japanese families.

In *My Neighbor Totoro*, ten-year-old Satsuki and her four-year-old sister, Mei, live alone with their father because their mother is ill in the hospital. Just before they meet the forest spirit that whisks them away from their dreary everyday lives, Satsuki prepares a bento for a picnic. The task of preparing this simple, appealing lunch is more meaningful than it appears: The bento represents the heavy burden the girl carries while she serves as the family's housewife.

INGREDIENTS

⅔ cup uncooked rice

2 frozen shishamo smelt

Olive oil for frying

3½ ounces snapper (or other white fish, such as tilapia)

1 teaspoon sake

2 tablespoons sugar

1 teaspoon salt

2 drops red food coloring

2 dried jujube fruits

30 edamame beans

DIFFICULTY: ● ● • • •

YIELD: 2 servings

TIME: 40 minutes

NOTE
Try your local Asian market for some of the harder-to-find ingredients used in this book, such as shishamo and nori.

DIRECTIONS

1 Cook the rice in a pot of water. While the rice is cooking, thaw the shishamo; then slide the fish into a frying pan over medium heat. Add a drizzle of olive oil and cook for 5 minutes; then flip the shishamo and cook for another 5 minutes. Remove the fish from the pan and place it on a paper towel to absorb any excess oil.

2 In a separate saucepan, boil some water and drop in the snapper. When the fish is slightly flaky, drain it and set it aside on a plate. (If you're using frozen snapper fillets, simply thaw them.)

3 Place the snapper fillets in a frying pan over medium heat; add the sake, sugar, and salt. Break up the fillets into small pieces and stir until all the liquid has evaporated.

4 Add the red food coloring and a little water to achieve the desired color; then lower the heat. Stir well.

5 Take out two bento boxes. Divide the rice in half and spoon one half into the large compartment of each bento box; also add one fried shishamo and one dried jujube to each box. Fill one small compartment with the snapper pieces and the other small compartment with the edamame.

ITADAKIMASU!

OKAYU

BACKGROUND

In the film *Princess Mononoke*, Ashitaka has been cursed by a demon. On his quest to lift the curse, he encounters forest spirits and the main character San, also known as Princess Mononoke. This medieval film by Hayao Miyazaki, set in medieval times, reflects the animist themes the director often returns to, including the importance of humans living in harmony with nature.

During his adventures, the young hero meets Jigo, a wandering monk. As the two eat together in the woods, the old man explains that they are actually sitting in the ruins of a village that the spirits destroyed.

The monk serves Ashitaka a sort of rice soup that he seasons with what could be miso paste. The porridge, called *okayu*, is usually given to children or people who are sick. *Okayu is* believed to have healing properties, particularly for stomachaches. It can be thickened with eggs and served with salmon, *umeboshi* (dried, pickled plums), and, as shown in the film, chives.

INGREDIENTS

4 eggs

2 teaspoons cornstarch

1 tablespoon miso*

1 tablespoon crushed chicken
  bouillon cubes

⅓ cup uncooked jasmine rice

1 to 3 sprigs cilantro, chopped

Pinch of pepper for garnish

Pinch of crispy fried onions for garnish

*Soy sauce may be substituted for miso in any
 of the recipes.

Note that soy sauce can contain gluten.

DIFFICULTY: ● ● • • •

YIELD: 2 servings

TIME: 40 minutes

DIRECTIONS

1 Boil 4 cups of water in a saucepan. Meanwhile, heat a pan and use one of the eggs to make an omelet: Beat the egg, cook it for 2 to 3 minutes over high heat, and then remove the egg from the pan and slice it into strips.

2 Beat together the remaining three eggs. Make a slurry by combining the cornstarch with an equal amount of cold water. Cut the miso into small pieces to help it melt more quickly. When the water in the saucepan is boiling, add the beaten eggs, cornstarch slurry, crushed chicken bouillon cubes, and miso.

3 In a separate pot, cook the rice in water for 15 minutes; then add the cooked rice to the broth and simmer to obtain a porridge.

4 Pour the porridge into bowls. Arrange the omelet strips on top and sprinkle with cilantro, pepper, and crispy fried onion.

OKAYU CAN BE MADE IN A VARIETY OF WAYS. THIS IS A MORE LAVISH VERSION THAN THE SIMPLE BOWL OF PORRIDGE SEEN IN THE FILM.

ITADAKIMASU!

POM POKO
Isao Takahata, 1994

HOMEMADE HAMBURGERS

BACKGROUND

In the 1994 film *Pom Poko*, human developments threaten to destroy the natural habitat of the *tanuki*, mischievous, carefree "raccoon dogs" that appear throughout Japanese folklore. At first, the *tanuki* adopt a wait-and-see approach. Eventually, however, they unite to fight the human invaders, celebrating their alliance with fat, juicy McDonald's hamburgers. The little carnivores think the burgers are absolutely delicious—and very high in nutritional value, too.

This McDonald's scene is intentionally ironic. Director Isao Takahata shows the animals smacking their lips at their taste of the modern lifestyle that will overrun their natural habitat as metropolitan Tokyo continues to expand.

McDonald's first opened in Japan in 1971, and although the fast-food chain is popular there, it is also seen as a symbol of industrialization and globalization. The burgers represent not only the onslaught of modern life against nature, but also the opposition of the Western world and Japanese tradition, embodied by the *tanuki*.

On the plus side, this recipe is a more nutritious (and tastier) version of the burgers shown in the film.

INGREDIENTS

6 ounces ground beef (or ground meat of choice)

1 egg

1 clove garlic, grated

½ teaspoon garlic powder

1 teaspoon paprika

1 tablespoon crushed chicken bouillon cubes

½ tablespoon fish sauce

½ teaspoon salt

½ teaspoon pepper

Parsley

½ onion, grated

1 tablespoon flour

Oil for frying

2 hamburger buns

DIFFICULTY: ✦ ✦ • • •

YIELD: 2 servings

TIME: 45 minutes

Condiments (ketchup, mustard, barbecue sauce, or other sauce of choice)

Lettuce leaves

1 tomato, sliced

1 onion, sliced

2 slices cheddar cheese

DIRECTIONS

1 In a large mixing bowl, thoroughly combine the ground beef, egg, grated garlic, garlic powder, paprika, crushed chicken bouillon cubes, fish sauce, salt, pepper, parsley (to taste), and grated onion. Add the flour. Knead the mixture and refrigerate for 30 minutes.

2 Heat a frying pan and add oil for frying. Take the meat mixture out of the refrigerator and divide the meat into two portions. Form each half into a ball; then flatten each ball into a patty with your hands and place both the patties in the oiled pan. Watch the patties closely, flipping them every 2 minutes until they reach your preferred doneness

3 Preheat the oven to 250ºF. Slice the buns in half and spread with your favorite condiments. Arrange one or two lettuce leaves, two or three tomato slices, and desired onion slices on the bottom of each bun. Add a meat patty and then a cheese slice, and cover the burger with the top of the bun.

4 Warm the assembled burgers in the oven for 5 minutes.

ITADAKIMASU!

WHEN MARNIE WAS THERE
Hiromasa Yonebayashi, 2014

SEAFOOD SALAD

BACKGROUND

When *Marnie Was There* tells the story of Anna, an unhappy orphan who is sent to the remote Hokkaido region to stay with her foster mother's family, the Oiwas. There Anna meets and befriends a ghostly girl named Marnie.

Back at the Oiwa home, Anna sits down to a typical meal served in the coastal region: salad accompanied by sashimi and a platter of shellfish. Over dinner, Anna's hosts tell her about the ghost that haunts the Marsh house, confirming that Anna's encounter was indeed a supernatural one.

Kiyomasa Oiwa, the father of the family, jokes about spirits while munching on tender pieces of kabocha squash pickled in soy sauce and mirin, a sweet and salty condiment called *kabocha no nimono*. The pickles in Yonebayashi's film are so soft that Kiyomasa can easily cut them with a chopstick.

INGREDIENTS

- 9 ounces cockles or littleneck clams, in the shell
- 9 ounces steamer clams, in the shell
- 9 ounces whelks, in the shell
- 9 ounces cooked shrimp
- 1 onion
- 1 lemon
- 6 large lettuce leaves
- 10 cherry tomatoes (or tomato slices)
- 15 black olives
- 5 ounces cheese cubes (such as gouda or edam)

DIFFICULTY: ● • • •

YIELD: 3 servings

TIME: 35 minutes

DIRECTIONS

1 In a saucepan, boil 4 cups of water; then drop in the cockles, steamer clams, and whelks. Cook for 15 to 20 minutes and drain the shellfish. While the shellfish are cooling, peel and cube the shrimp and place them in a bowl.

2 Dice the onion and add it to the bowl. Halve the lemon, squeeze the juice from one half into the bowl, and stir.

3 Separate and wash the lettuce leaves. Use a teaspoon to scoop the shrimp salad into the lettuce leaves. Squeeze the other lemon half over the top of the shrimp salad.

4 Arrange the lettuce leaves on a platter with the tomatoes, olives, and cheese cubes, and serve with the shellfish.

ITADAKIMASU!

TALES FROM EARTHSEA
Goro Miyazaki, 2006

VEGETABLE SOUP

BACKGROUND

*T*ales from Earthsea is an adaptation of Ursula K. Le Guin's fantasy book series, which follows the adventures of the archmage Sparrowhawk and Prince Arren, who has fled his kingdom after killing his father, the king. Horrified by what he has done, Arren gets lost in his thoughts and is captured by slave traders. Sparrowhawk eventually rescues him.

To give the young prince time to recover emotionally, the archmage asks his old friend Tenar to shelter them. In the middle of the night, Tenar takes them in and serves them soup from a large pot. This soup appears to be a Mediterranean dish made of root vegetables, olives, and tomatoes. The arid landscapes of Earthsea visually evoke a similar region, as does Sparrowhawk's wanderer type of appearance.

Beyond providing sustenance to the travelers, this simple fireside supper embodies the close, warm friendship between Sparrowhawk and Tenar, who have not seen each other in five years.

INGREDIENTS

1 leek

1 white radish

2 carrots

1 zucchini

1 onion

3 tablespoons olive oil

Pinch of ground turmeric

Salt and pepper

6 cups hot water

1 tablespoon crushed chicken
   bouillon cubes

$\frac{1}{3}$ cup peas

20 olives

1 ounce rice vermicelli

14 ounces tomato sauce

1 tablespoon parsley, chopped

1 tablespoon cilantro, chopped

DIFFICULTY:  • • • •

YIELD: 4 servings

TIME: 40 minutes

DIRECTIONS

1 Slice the leek, radish, carrots, zucchini, and onion into rounds.

2 Pour the olive oil into a large pot, and then add the leek and onion. Cover and cook over medium heat for 3 minutes.

3   Add the carrots, zucchini, radish, and turmeric to the pot. Season to taste with salt and pepper, and stir.

4   Add the hot water along with the crushed chicken bouillon cubes, peas, and olives. Cover and cook the soup for 20 minutes. Meanwhile, soak the rice vermicelli in cold water to soften, and then divide it among 4 bowls.

5 Add the tomato sauce, parsley, and cilantro to the pot, and stir. Cook for another 5 minutes. Ladle the soup over the noodles and serve.

ITADAKIMASU!

HOWL'S
BACON & EGGS

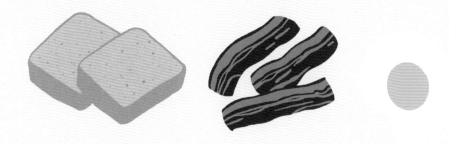

BACKGROUND

In *Howl's Moving Castle*, after meeting the wizard Howl, Sophie is cursed by a witch who steals her youth and transforms her into an old woman. Sophie finds refuge in the moving castle, Howl's magical fortress, by claiming to be a cleaning lady.

Even when Sophie prepares breakfast for Howl and his apprentice, the wizard does not recognize her true identity. Meaning to spare an old woman some work, Howl takes a pan of bacon and eggs from Sophie. As he does so, their hands brush. The touch stirs something in the young girl.

The film's setting is decidedly European, and the meal is a traditional, hearty English breakfast served with rye bread and cheese. Sophie can't talk about the spell she is under, so she simply polishes off her entire meal and then gives the castle a thorough cleaning, to let off some steam.

INGREDIENTS

2 slices bacon

Olive oil for cooking (or cooking oil
of choice)

2 eggs

½ teaspoon garlic powder (or to taste)

Salt and pepper

1 slice sandwich bread, crust removed

DIFFICULTY: ❀ ❀ • • •

YIELD: 1 serving

TIME: 15 minutes

DIRECTIONS

1 In an oiled pan, fry the bacon slices on each side until crispy. Set aside.

2 Beat the eggs with the garlic powder (feel free to add less than the full ½ teaspoon, if desired), adding salt and pepper to taste.

3 Cut the slice of bread in half.

4 Pour the eggs into the hot pan and place the bread slices in the center. Flip the bread immediately so that both sides are coated.

5 When the eggs have solidified, fold all four sides of the omelet toward the center of the pan.

6 Cut the cooked bacon slices into pieces and arrange them on the omelet.

7 Quickly fold the omelet in half to form a sandwich, with a slice of bread on each side.

ITADAKIMASU!

SPIRITED AWAY
Hayao Miyazaki, 2001

TUNA ONIGIRI

BACKGROUND

S*pirited Away*, a film by Hayao Miyazaki, is the second-highest-grossing Japanese film worldwide. It tells the adventures of Chihiro, a little girl trapped in an *onsen* (bathhouse) run by spirits from Japanese folklore.

When the girl's parents accidentally enter the supernatural realm and begin eating from a mouthwatering buffet without permission, the spirits transform them into pigs. Chihiro does not eat any of the food, so she avoids their fate and is rescued by a mysterious boy, Haku, who finds her a job at the bathhouse. To help her recover, he gives her an enchanted *onigiri* that restores her strength and prevents her from turning into a pig.

Onigiri are the ultimate Japanese street food: balls of rice generally shaped into triangles and wrapped in a piece of nori. They are typically filled with fish, pickled *umeboshi* plums, or a wide variety of meats or condiments. Filling and relatively healthy, the simple *onigiri* contrasts with the rich foods scarfed down by Chihiro's parents.

INGREDIENTS

1 cup uncooked jasmine rice

4 tablespoons distilled white vinegar

1 teaspoon salt (or to taste)

2 teaspoons sugar (or to taste)

One 5-ounce can tuna

1 tablespoon mayonnaise (or more,
to taste)

4 strips toasted nori

DIFFICULTY: ●● • • •

YIELD: 4 servings

TIME: 30 minutes

DIRECTIONS

1 Add the rice to a pot and rinse thoroughly until the water runs clear; then pour in enough water to cover the rice by about half an inch. Cook the rice.

2 Pour the vinegar over the cooked rice. Add the salt and sugar, and stir (feel free to use less salt and sugar, if desired).

3 Break up the tuna in a bowl, and thoroughly mix in the mayonnaise (feel free to use more than 1 tablespoon, if desired).

4 Wet your hands and form four cakes of rice. Spread a flat layer of tuna over each, and then cover with another flat cake of rice. Shape the filled rice into balls, and mold the corners to form triangles.

5 Moisten the nori strips and wrap them around the *onigiri*.

ITADAKIMASU!

FROM UP ON POPPY HILL
Goro Miyazaki, 2011

SHRIMP
TEMPURA

BACKGROUND

In the 2001 film *From Up on Poppy Hill*, Umi is a responsible high school student who lives in the hills above Yokohama. While her mother is away working at a university, Umi takes care of her brothers, sisters, and grandmother. She manages the family boardinghouse and prepares traditional Japanese meals for all the lodgers. In one scene, Umi makes shrimp tempura that sound light and crispy when she sets them on a plate. These tasty Japanese delicacies are generally fried in sesame oil. They can be enjoyed by themselves or served in a noodle soup called tempura udon.

Tempura is not always made with shrimp; it is also commonly prepared with vegetables and a wide variety of fish and seafood. Although this Japanese specialty was originally inspired by a recipe introduced by Portuguese sailors, it features a uniquely light, crispy coating of fried wheat flour (called *tenkasu*). The way Umi calmly moves the tempura around in the boiling oil with her chopsticks demonstrates her maturity and her comfort with cooking.

INGREDIENTS

Sesame oil for frying (or other frying
  oil of choice)

10 raw shrimp

1 egg

¾ cup cold water

1 cup flour

Panko breadcrumbs

DIFFICULTY: 🦠 • • • •

YIELD: 2 servings

TIME: 15 minutes

SHRIMP TEMPURA ❖ *FROM UP ON POPPY HILL*

DIRECTIONS

1 Heat the frying oil in a deep pan. While the oil is heating, peel the shrimp and beat together the egg and cold water in a bowl. Sift the flour onto a plate, and pour the breadcrumbs onto a separate plate.

2 Roll each shrimp in flour, hold them by the tail to dip them in the beaten egg, and then roll them in the breadcrumbs.

3 Drop the shrimp into the hot oil and fry them on both sides. The breading should be golden brown on each side. Tip: Set the tempura on paper towels to absorb excess oil before serving

THIS RECIPE ALSO WORKS FOR FRYING OTHER INGREDIENTS (SLICES OF RAW FISH, CUTTLEFISH, OCTOPUS, CARROTS, AND SO ON).

ITADAKIMASU!

PONYO
Hayao Miyazaki, 2008

RAMEN

BACKGROUND

*P*onyo follows the adventures of Ponyo, a fish with a human head who is the daughter of a wizard and an ocean deity. After she meets five-year-old Sōsuke, a human boy, Ponyo becomes a little girl who knows nothing of the on-land world and eats only one food: ham. Sōsuke's mother serves her ramen, a Japanese soup with long, thin noodles.

Traditional ramen broth may be either clear or cloudy, and the soup may be topped with a variety of ingredients, including fish, meat, soft-boiled eggs, mushrooms, seaweed, and spices. This inexpensive dish is often eaten at the counter of little stands called *yatai*.

Sōsuke's mother does not make home-cooked ramen; instead, she uses instant noodle packets. She does promise the children a surprise, however: She adds soft-boiled eggs, pork, and green onions to the bowls to make them look fancier. Like a toddler, Ponyo expresses all the endearing emotions of trying something new: impatience, joy, and sleepiness after eating.

INGREDIENTS

8 cups water, divided

1 cube chicken bouillon

1 tablespoon crushed chicken bouillon cubes

3 tablespoons soy sauce, divided

2 tablespoons mirin

1 teaspoon oyster sauce

1 tablespoon sugar

4 garlic cloves, divided

Olive oil for cooking (or cooking oil of choice)

9 ounces pork (such as boneless ribs)

2 fresh eggs

1 packet ramen noodles

1 leek

Pinch of fresh ginger, grated or thinly sliced

DIFFICULTY: ✺✺✺ • •

YIELD: 2 servings

TIME: 45 minutes

1¼ cup soy milk

1 onion

2 green onions

Salt and pepper

Optional: 1 tablespoon white miso paste

DIRECTIONS

1 In a saucepan, boil 4 cups of the water. Add the bouillon cube, crushed chicken bouillon cubes, and 1 tablespoon of the soy sauce (or miso paste, if using). Taste often and adjust the seasoning as you go, gradually adding more crushed chicken bouillon cubes or soy sauce (or miso paste, if using) to taste.

2 While the broth warms, prepare the marinade: Pour the remaining soy sauce into a bowl and add the mirin, oyster sauce, and sugar. Stir well.

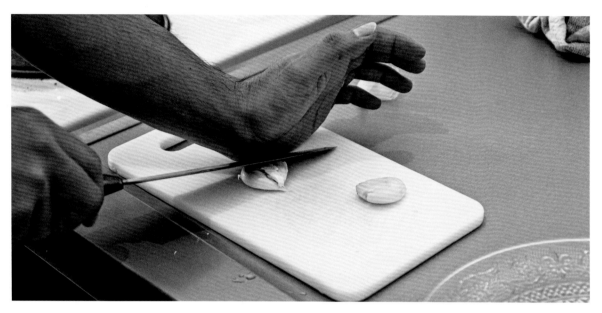

3 Smash three garlic cloves with the flat side of your knife, and then thinly slice them. Add the garlic to the marinade.

4 Oil a pan and cook the pork on both sides until it is completely white. Remove the pork from the pan and thinly slice the meat. Add the marinade to the pan and then add the sliced meat. Fry on both sides.

5 Cook the eggs in a pot of boiling water for 6 minutes, then drain and peel. In a separate pot, cook the noodles until soft. Divide the noodles between 2 bowls.

6 Wash the leek and cut the white part into rounds. Chop the remaining garlic clove. Add the leek rounds to the broth, along with the ginger, the soy milk, and the remaining chopped garlic clove.

7 While the broth cooks, cutthe onion and green onion into thin strips, and halve theboiled eggs.

8 Pour the broth over the noodles in the bowls. Garnish with the egg halves and slices of pork, and sprinkle the onion and green onion on top. Season with salt and pepper, and serve.

ITADAKIMASU!

THE TALE OF THE PRINCESS KAGUYA
Isao Takahata, 2013

MUSHROOM & CHICKEN STIR-FRY

BACKGROUND

In *The Tale of Princess Kaguya*, peasants find a young Kaguya in a bamboo shoot and raise her as their daughter. The little girl flourishes in her simple country life and makes friends with the village children during her rapid three-month development into a grown woman.

During a pheasant hunt, sparks of romance fly between Kaguya and a young man named Sutemaru. Kaguya finds some mushrooms to cook with the pheasant, and the children agree to make a stir-fry the next day. Unfortunately, they never get to share the meal because Kaguya's father decides that she deserves a more noble upbringing. He takes her to live in a castle, where she is to become a princess. This missed rendezvous with friends is a central tragedy of the film.

In the city, far from her friends, Kaguya experiences the splendors of a life of privilege, but she enjoys no personal freedom and loses her sense of joy. Her abandoned frugal meal with her friends, consisting of some stir-fried mushrooms and poultry, comes to symbolize Kaguya's removal from a simple country life. This recipe adaptation would surely remind Kaguya of her youth's joyful memories.

INGREDIENTS

9 ounces chicken (or other poultry)

3 cloves garlic

1 tablespoon sesame oil

1 tablespoon soy sauce

1 egg

Salt and pepper

¾ cup uncooked rice

9 ounces mushrooms (white mushrooms or a blend)

2 tablespoons unsalted butter

1 tablespoon olive oil

DIFFICULTY: ⬤⬤ • • •

YIELD: 3 servings

TIME: 30 minutes

DIRECTIONS

1 Cut the chicken into small pieces. Chop the garlic and divide it into two equal portions.

2 Put half of the garlic in a mixing bowl with the chicken pieces, sesame oil, soy sauce, egg, salt, and pepper. Stir well, and then refrigerate for about 10 minutes. Meanwhile, cook the rice in boiling water for 15 minutes.

3 While the rice is cooking, slice the mushrooms.

4 In a frying pan, melt the butter and then add the olive oil and the remaining garlic. Sauté until the garlic turns yellow. Add the mushrooms and fry them, turning once in the middle of cooking.

5 Remove the marinated chicken from the refrigerator and add it to the pan. Brown the chicken on all sides. Serve with the rice.

ITADAKIMASU!

CASTLE IN THE SKY
Hayao Miyazaki, 1986

BEEF STEW

BACKGROUND

Sheeta, an innocent girl who holds secrets about a castle in the sky, is pursued by nefarious forces seeking those secrets. At the beginning of the film, a band of pirates attacks Sheeta. Ultimately, they become her substitute family, and the boorish Captain Dola takes on a motherly role. The relationship between Sheeta and Dola evolves aboard the pirates' ship, where the girl is sent to cook in the filthy galley. Dola informs Sheeta that she must serve five meals a day and barks, "Economize on the water!"

Given those instructions, it's no surprise to see that the first meal Sheeta prepares onboard is an enormous pot of stew filled with meat, potatoes, and carrots. Sheeta herself doesn't appear particularly tired: She has enlisted the pirates—who have collectively fallen in love with her—to peel, scrub, and prep. As they work together to prepare the family dinner, Dola's crew transforms into a group of harmless nitwits.

INGREDIENTS

1 pound stew beef, such as chuck roast

4 carrots

3 onions

10 medium waxy potatoes

Sea salt for boiling water

2 cups uncooked rice

¼ cup veal stock

2 tablespoons unsalted butter

Olive oil for frying

¾ cup flour

½ cup red wine

3 tablespoons white miso paste

1 bouquet garni (thyme and bay leaf)

14 ounces tomato sauce

Salt and pepper

DIFFICULTY: ✺✺✺ • •

YIELD: 8 servings

TIME: 5 hours, 45 minutes

DIRECTIONS

1 Cut the meat into large cubes. Peel the carrots and onions, and slice them into rounds. Divide the carrot rounds into two equal portions. Peel and quarter the potatoes.

2 Drop the potatoes and half of the carrots into a saucepan of boiling, salted water. In another saucepan, prepare the rice by boiling in water for 15 minutes. In a third saucepan, heat 4 cups of water and add the veal stock. Bring to a boil.

3 Warm the butter and olive oil in a large stewpot over medium heat. Add the cubes of meat, and brown on each side.

4 Remove the meat to a plate, sprinkle with the flour, and set aside.

5 Brown the remaining carrots and the onions in the same stewpot; then remove them and set aside.

6 Pour the oil out of the stewpot, and deglaze with the wine. Put the meat back into the stewpot, along with the white miso paste, browned carrots and onions, bouquet garni, tomato sauce, and broth from the third saucepan..

7 Add the potatoes and carrots from the first saucepan to the stewpot. Season with salt and pepper. Cover and simmer over low heat for 4 to 5 hours. Serve with the rice.

SPAGHETTI WITH MEATBALLS

BACKGROUND

*P*orco Rosso is a fanciful film set in 1920s Italy that exhibits the exotic flair of Japanese director Hayao Miyazaki. Pilot Marco is transformed into a pig while flying his seaplane. After he lands, he must have his plane repaired by a man named Paolo Piccolo. Marco meets Paolo's granddaughter, Fio, and other female relatives who are performing the repairs, and he joins them for a lunch of spaghetti and red wine. The family begins the simple, traditional meal by saying grace, but Porco abstains from the prayer, showing his disillusionment and lack of faith.

While the women are preparing the meal, Paolo explains to Marco that the Great Depression has forced all the men to emigrate to find work. He adds, however, as the meal is served, "Women are good. They work well and have guts." Marco, who's about to take a bite of his pasta, answers, "Making an airplane isn't the same as cooking pancakes." Ultimately, the scene is not about pasta at all, but instead centers on the role of women in Italian society during that era. These days, of course, this traditional Italian dish can be prepared by anyone—man or woman!

INGREDIENTS

12 ounces uncooked spaghetti

A few sprigs parsley

2 cloves garlic

7 ounces ground meat (preferably pork)

1 teaspoon grated ginger

Pinch of garlic powder

1 tablespoon paprika

1 tablespoon crushed chicken bouillon cubes

2 eggs

2 tomatoes

14 ounces tomato sauce

DIFFICULTY: ✿ ✿ • • •

YIELD: 2 servings

TIME: 25 minutes

DIRECTIONS

1 Boil water in a large saucepan and cook the spaghetti according to the package directions (approximately 10 minutes). Drain the spaghetti and set aside.

2 While the spaghetti cooks, chop the parsley and garlic.

3 Put the ground meat into a mixing bowl with the parsley (to taste), chopped garlic, ginger, garlic powder, paprika, crushed chicken bouillon cubes, and eggs. Knead to combine.

4 Roll the meat mixture into balls that fit into the palm of your hand. Brown them on all sides in a frying pan, and then remove the balls and set them aside.

5 Cube the tomatoes. Over low heat, stir the cooked spaghetti with the tomato sauce and chopped tomatoes in the pan used to cook the meatballs for at least a minute.

6 Serve the spaghetti in bowls topped with the meatballs.

ITADAKIMASU!

MY NEIGHBORS THE YAMADAS
Isao Takahata, 1999

BEEF STROGANOFF

BACKGROUND

In the film *My Neighbors the Yamadas*, director Isao Takahata presents a humorous, caricatured picture of a modern Japanese family through a series of vignettes.

Matsuko Yamada, the mother, is often the target of jokes decrying her lack of creativity and motivation in cooking, which clashes with the popular image of Japanese mothers as accomplished chefs. In the episode "The Perfect Combo," Matsuko is craving a plate of sushi. She pretends to be ordering it in, hoping that her mother, Shige, will offer to make it. As expected, the old woman complains that it's too expensive and offers to make the sushi herself.

In the kitchen, however, Shige changes her mind and tries to make beef stroganoff. Unfortunately, she doesn't know how to pronounce the dish, let alone cook it! After failing to make the stroganoff over a lengthy period of time, Shige finally says, "No good, I screwed it up. Order the sushi."

Beef stroganoff, originally a Russian dish, is not particularly hard to make, but it's too difficult for Shige, who is no more a chef than her daughter. This recipe, however, is simple *and* delicious.

INGREDIENTS

Olive oil for frying

½ onion, sliced

10 ounces beef

1 teaspoon paprika

Salt and pepper

¼ cup dry white wine

¼ cup cream

1 teaspoon ground mustard

DIFFICULTY: 🖤 • • •

YIELD: 2 servings

TIME: 15 minutes

DIRECTIONS

1 Lightly oil the pan and warm over high heat. Add the sliced onion.

2 Cut the beef into strips.

3 When the onion begins to brown, arrange the meat in the pan, evenly spaced, and sprinkle it with paprika, salt, and pepper. Brown both sides until the meat is cooked to your taste. Deglaze with the white wine and cook to reduce.

4 Lower the heat, pour in the cream, and reduce again, taking care not to burn the cream. Remove the pan from the heat.

5 Stir the mustard through the sauce. Spoon onto two plates and serve.

ITADAKIMASU!

SHELLFISH PLATTER WITH RICE

BACKGROUND

Grave of the Fireflies tells the heartbreaking tale of two orphans, fourteen-year-old Seita and his four-year-old sister, Setsuko. The two are left to fend for themselves and eventually succumb to starvation. In this tragic yet lyrical film by Isao Takahata, food is of central importance.

After being slowly starved by a cruel aunt who steals most of their meager resources, the children leave to live by themselves in a bomb shelter, where they reclaim their childhood and create a semblance of home. To celebrate their new adventure, they work together to cook what ends up being their final feast. They catch seafood in a river, boil a turnip, and serve it with the most exciting dish imaginable during a war: white rice. Seita and Setsuko laugh and revel in the joy of eating at a proper table.

The director shows the dishes completely empty, and despite the ample meal, the children are already thinking about eating frogs, which hints at how malnourished they are.

INGREDIENTS

3 tablespoons soy sauce

2 tablespoons mirin

1 tablespoon sesame oil

½ lemon, juiced

1 teaspoon white miso paste

3 cloves garlic

1½ ounces steamer clams

1½ ounces whelks

15 ounces cockles or littleneck clams

Salt

$\frac{2}{3}$ cup uncooked rice

1 onion

2 green onions

1 tablespoon olive oil

DIFFICULTY: ● ● • • •

YIELD: 2 servings

TIME: 45 minutes

DIRECTIONS

1 Add the soy sauce, mirin, sesame oil, lemon juice, and white miso paste to a mixing bowl. Thinly slice the garlic and stir it into the marinade;
set aside.

2 Rinse the shellfish and place it in a large bowl of water for 5 to 10 minutes.

3 Boil 3 cups of water in a saucepan. Drain the shellfish, add it to the saucepan, pour in enough water to cover it, and salt. Cook for 10 minutes, and drain again.

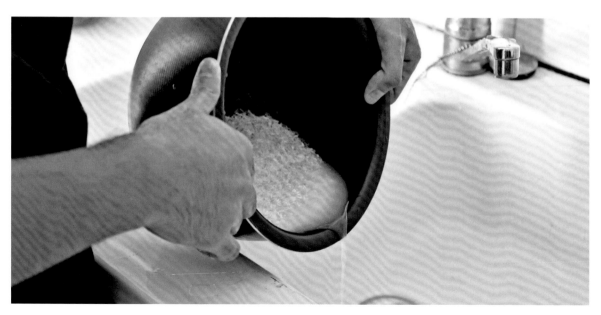

4 In a separate saucepan, cook the rice for 15 minutes.

5 Slice the onion and green onions into rounds.

6 Heat a pan, and then add the olive oil. Add the shellfish to the pan and pour the marinade over the top. Fry.

7 Add the onion and green onion. Cover the pan and simmer for 10 minutes over low heat. Serve the rice on plates alongside the shellfish.

ITADAKIMASU!

HERRING & PUMPKIN PIE

BACKGROUND

In *Kiki's Delivery Service*, thirteen-year-old Kiki leaves home to complete her apprenticeship as a witch. Being on her own for the first time in a new city is challenging, but the young witch decides to earn a living by making deliveries—on her broomstick. Kiki receives a call from Madame, an elderly woman who wants Kiki to deliver a homecooked meal to her granddaughter for her birthday. Unfortunately, Madame's oven is not working, and she can't bake her usual herring and pumpkin pie. Unwilling to accept payment without making the delivery, Kiki helps Madame bake the pie, even though it means missing a party.

The pie is rustic and clearly made with love, but the delivery is a disappointment: Instead of thanking Kiki, the granddaughter complains, "I hate Grandma's stupid pies."

The story takes place in an imaginary European city, and the dish is probably meant to be a regional specialty that the grandmother is known for making. As an added touch, witches are often associated with pumpkins, so including that ingredient in the pie is likely a nod to the cliché.

INGREDIENTS

¼ pumpkin or 1 butternut squash,
   depending on the season

20 black olives, pitted

2 cloves garlic

1 medium white onion

¼ teaspoon salt

1/8 teaspoon pepper

Pinch of paprika

2 tablespoons salted butter

1 tablespoon olive oil

¾ cup plus 2 tablespoons cream

4 smoked herring fillets

2 pie crusts, uncooked

1 egg yolk, beaten

DIFFICULTY: 😊 😊 😊 • •

YIELD: 6 servings

TIME: 1 hour, 10 minutes

DIRECTIONS

1 Scoop the seeds out of the pumpkin, cube the flesh, and steam for approximately 20 minutes.

2 Thinly slice 10 olives, chop the garlic, and slice the onion into rounds.

3 When the pumpkin is soft, remove it from heat and mash it into a purée. Add the salt, pepper, paprika, butter, and olives.

4 Lightly brown the garlic and onion in the oil. Add the cream, and stir to combine. Warm the mixture, and then pour in the pumpkin purée. Stir to combine.

5 Spread the mixture into the bottom of a pie pan in a flat, even layer.

6 Preheat the oven to 350°F. Cut the smoked herring into small pieces, and arrange them on top of the purée, evenly spaced.

7 Cover the contents of the pie with one pie crust. Then cut thin strips from the other pie crust (or from scraps of the first) to lay over the whole crust, as shown in the photo.

8 If desired, you can recreate the fish from the film by cutting out its shape and scalesfrom another piece of pie crust and then placing those pieces on top of the strips.

9 Use a knife tip to poke 10 small cross-shaped holes around the edges of the pie on top of the crust strips. Brush the entire crust with egg yolk. Place the remaining 10 olives in the holes for decoration.

10 Bake the pie for 40 minutes at 350°F.

ITADAKIMASU!

DESSERTS

RED BEAN BUNS

BACKGROUND

While working in a supernatural bathhouse, Chihiro manages to free the spirit of a polluted river. In appreciation, the spirit gives her a strange dumpling. Chihiro tucks away the dumpling and then sits down with her co-worker, Lin, to eat an *anpan* after her hard day of work.

These sweet buns, which are as common in Japan as donuts are in America, are traditionally filled with red bean paste, but an *anpan* can also have a sesame or chestnut filling. The bun in the film is almost as big as Chihiro's face, and she seems to be making a meal of it.

Chihiro also tastes the strange dumpling, which makes her hair stand on end. She chases away the taste with another bite of *anpan*. Later, she uses the gift to release a spirit called No-Face from its voracious appetite. Balance is important in the Japanese diet, and *Spirited Away* repeatedly touches on the theme of gluttony. Whenever characters overeat, they are punished. Luckily for you, there's no need to worry about punishment from overeating these delicious Red Bean Buns!

INGREDIENTS

½ cup milk

1 tablespoon active dry yeast

1⅔ cup flour, divided

Pinch of baking powder

Pinch of salt

2½ teaspoons sugar

18 ounces red bean paste

0.07 ounces (2 grams) agar-agar powder

Olive oil to prevent sticking

Equipment: Steamer

DIFFICULTY: ● ● ● ● •

YIELD: 3 servings

TIME: 3 hours

DIRECTIONS

1 Add the milk, yeast, 1 cup of flour, baking powder, salt, and sugar to a large mixing bowl, and stir thoroughly to form a soft dough.

2 Turn out the dough onto a floured work surface, and sprinkle generously with flour. Roll out the dough, add more flour as needed, and so on. Continue to work the dough for 10 to 15 minutes.

3 When you stretch the dough, you should be able to see light through it without it tearing. When you reach this stage, form the dough into a ball, place it in a container, cover it, and set aside in a warm place for 1½ hours.

4 While the dough is resting, add the red bean paste and agar powder to a saucepan, along with enough water to cover the paste. Warm over medium heat, stirring constantly, until the water has evaporated. Let cool.

5 Take out the ball of dough, spread it out into a rectangle on your floured work surface, and then roll it into a log. Divide the dough into three large pieces to form the buns.

6 Pinch the tops of each bun, and roll each piece to make smooth, round balls. Cover for 20 minutes.

7 Flatten the dough balls with a rolling pin so that the edges are thicker and the center is thinner. Spoon the red bean paste mixture onto each dough round. Fold up the edges neatly, to close the buns. Coat your fingers with olive oil, and then twist the tops of the buns to seal them.

8 Place the buns on parchment paper with the sealed side down, and let rest for 10 minutes.

9 Steam the buns for 10 minutes.

SHORTBREAD COOKIES

BACKGROUND

In *Whisper of the Heart*, Shizuku ponders her future against the backdrop of a romance with Seiji, an apprentice luthier. Having made up her mind to seize her own destiny and take some risks, Shizuku announces over snacks with her best friend, Yuko, that she plans to write a novel.

The two friends sit at a table sipping cups of tea and nibbling on cookies, some of which are round and look like shortbread. The other snacks are clearly Pocky, chocolate-coated biscuit sticks that are an iconic Japanese snack food.

Pocky were first sold in Japan in 1966, but they didn't arrive in the United States until 2003. The classic flavors include milk chocolate, strawberry, and matcha, but many other varieties of Pocky are sold today.

Shortbread cookies, on the other hand, have a Scottish origin: Mary, Queen of Scots, is credited with popularizing them in the 1500s. These sweet cookies were expensive to make during that era and were eaten only during special occasions, such as Christmas or weddings. Fortunately, shortbread cookies are both plentiful and affordable today, and this recipe is the perfect snack for anyone.

INGREDIENTS

6 tablespoons (90 grams) salted butter, softened

5 tablespoons (60 grams) sugar

½ teaspoon vanilla extract

1 egg yolk

1¼ cup (150 grams) flour

DIFFICULTY: ● ● • • •

YIELD: 2 servings

TIME: 2 hours

DIRECTIONS

1 Add the butter, sugar, and vanilla to a mixing bowl, and cream together until well blended.

2 Beat in the egg yolk.

3 Thoroughly mix in the flour. When the ingredients come together to form a dough, knead it into a ball using your hands.

4 Place the dough in a covered bowl and refrigerate it for 90 minutes. After the dough has chilled, use a rolling pin to roll it out between two sheets of parchment paper.

5 Remove the top sheet of parchment paper, and use a cookie cutter to cut pieces of dough in any shape you choose.

6 Preheat the oven to 350°F. Bake the cookies for about 10 minutes, depending on their size. Let the cookies cool before serving.

ITADAKIMASU!

JAM COOKIES

BACKGROUND

In *The Secret World of Arrietty*, tiny beings called the Borrowers live frugal lives pilfering small items from the human world. Shō, an ailing human boy awaiting heart surgery, unexpectedly crosses paths with one of these Borrowers, a teenage girl named Arrietty.

The chance encounter between Shō and Arrietty, who find kinship through their common loneliness, causes the Borrower family to move away. While Arrietty's family is looking for a new home, her father is injured; Spiller, another Borrower, comes to his aid. To thank Spiller, the family invites him to join them for tea, with accompanying jam cookies, in the dollhouse they have long called home.

Spiller lives in the wild, however, and he prefers his cricket haunch to the tea he is served. This contrast between refined dishes and simple fare reflects two very different lifestyles in the film: nomadic and sedentary. The next time you have guests, you can make your own jam cookies; they'll surely be received better than Arrietty's were.

INGREDIENTS

2 cups (250 grams) flour

1 cup (125 grams) powdered sugar

1 teaspoon baking powder

½ cup unsalted butter, at room temperature

1 egg yolk

1 teaspoon vanilla extract

¼ teaspoon salt

6 heaping tablespoons jam of your choice

DIFFICULTY: ❀ ❀ ❀ • •

YIELD: 2 servings

TIME: 1 hour, 30 minutes

DIRECTIONS

1 In a mixing bowl, sift together the flour and powdered sugar to prevent lumps. Add the baking powder, and stir.

2 Cut the butter into small cubes, mashing and kneading it into the dry ingredients.

3 Beat the egg with the vanilla, and add it to the mixture along with the salt. Knead until the dough forms a smooth ball, and then refrigerate the dough for 1 hour.

4 Preheat the oven to 300°F. Remove the dough from the refrigerator. Dust your work surface with flour, ad roll out the dough to a thickness of about $1/8$ inch. Use a cookie cutter to cut shapes from the dough.

5 Bake the cookies for 10 minutes, making sure they do not brown or overbake. The cookies should remain soft and light in color.

6 Remove the cookies from the oven and let them cool. Add the jam and, if desired, top with additional powdered sugar.

ITADAKIMASU!

THE CAT RETURNS
Hiroyuki Morita, 2002

VANILLA
SPONGE CAKE

BACKGROUND

I n *The Cat Returns*, Haru, a Japanese high schooler, saves a cat from being hit by a passing truck. That cat turns out to be Lune, the prince of the Cat Kingdom. To thank Haru, the grateful cats offer her Lune's hand in marriage. Looking for a way out of the arrangement, Haru visits the Cat Bureau and meets the Baron, a slender feline of British refinement who wears a top hat and a tailcoat.

The Baron invites Haru to tea and, in true English style, asks if she prefers milk or lemon. He also serves a vanilla sponge cake.

Afternoon tea is a quintessentially British ritual that generally features an array of sweet or savory finger foods. Traditionally, the meal includes egg or cucumber sandwiches, sponge cake, and scones. Just like in the Cat Kingdom, the goodies are also served with clotted cream.

In the film, Haru begins to shrink shortly after the tea scene, calling to mind the cake that makes Alice grow in the film *Alice in Wonderland*.

INGREDIENTS

3 ounces cream cheese

2 tablespoons salted butter

¼ cup milk

3 eggs

¼ cup (35 grams) flour

4 teaspoons cornstarch

½ teaspoon vanilla extract

¼ cup (55 grams) sugar

DIFFICULTY: ● ● • • •

YIELD: 4 servings

TIME: 1 hour, 35 minutes

DIRECTIONS

1 Melt the cream cheese, butter, and milk in a saucepan over low heat, stirring to obtain a thick liquid texture. Then remove the saucepan from heat.

2 Separate the egg yolks and whites into two different mixing bowls. Beat the egg yolks, pour them into the mixture in the saucepan, and stir to combine.

3 Sift the flour and cornstarch into the saucepan. Add the vanilla extract, and stir.

4 Beat the egg whites until frothy, pouring in the sugar one-third at a time until the texture is light and creamy. Important note: Do not overbeat the egg whites, or the cake might end up dry; the egg whites should be neither too dense nor too runny.

5 Fold the beaten egg whites into the batter, and stir.

6 Preheat the oven to 250°F. Grease a round cake pan and then pour in the batter. Place the cake pan into a larger dish containing warm water to create a double boiler. Place the entire dish in the oven, and bake at 250°F for 20 minutes, 300°F for 20 minutes, 230°F for 30 minutes, and then 350°F for 5 minutes.

7 Take the cake out of the oven, and remove it from the pan to cool.

ITADAKIMASU!

NAUSICAÄ OF THE VALLEY OF THE WIND
Hayao Miyazaki, 1984

NUT CAKE

NUT CAKE ❖ *NAUSICAÄ OF THE VALLEY OF THE WIND*

BACKGROUND

*N*ausicaä of the Valley of the Wind is set in a postapocalyptic world where humans struggle to survive on the inhospitable planet Earth. Nausicaä, the princess of the Valley of the Wind, tries her best to help humanity while navigating warring kingdoms and the needless battle between humans and nature.

At one point, Nausicaä rescues Asbel, a prince with a thirst for vengeance. The two discover that the air below the Toxic Jungle is clean. As they rest in the hidden oasis, Nausicaä shares with Asbel the *chiko* nuts given to her by some children. To someone who is trying to understand nature, not fight it, these nuts represent the gift of a sick planet. Asbel thinks the nuts taste awful, but these seeds of hope prove that Earth is not completely infertile.

Nausicaä tells Asbel that the nuts are healthy, and he gulps down a handful, symbolizing his gradual warming to Nausicaä's cause. This nut cake recipe is inspired by their sweet encounter.

INGREDIENTS

9 ounces mixed nuts (cashews, almonds, peanuts, and others)

4 eggs

1¼ cup (250 grams) granulated sugar

½ cup (125 grams) unsalted butter, softened

⅔ cup milk

2 teaspoons baking powder

1½ cup (180 grams) flour

DIFFICULTY: ● ● · · ·

YIELD: 6 servings

TIME: 1 hour

DIRECTIONS

1 Put the nuts in a plastic bag. Using a rolling pin, crush them inside the bag, taking care not to lose any nut powder.

2 Separate the egg yolks and whites into two different bowls. In a mixing bowl, stir together the sugar, butter, and egg yolks until fully combined. Add the milk, nuts, baking powder, and flour. Stir until the mixture thickens.

3 Beat the egg whites until frothy. Using a spatula, delicately fold them into the batter one half at a time, taking care not to deflate them.

4 Preheat the oven to 350°F. Pour the cake batter into a greased and/or floured cake pan of your choice, and bake for 40 minutes. Let cool before serving.

ITADAKIMASU!

THE WIND RISES
Hayao Miyazaki, 2013

SIBERIA SPONGE CAKE

BACKGROUND

In this biography inspired by the life of aeronautical engineer Jiro Horikoshi, the main character's fanatical obsession with flight keeps his attention focused on airplanes. Even Horikoshi's daydreams offer no escape: He envisions airplane wings among the bones of a herring.

One evening, Horikoshi encounters some children who are waiting for their parents to return. Jiro offers them slices of the Siberia cake he has just bought from a market stall, but the children are frightened and refuse. Horikoshi's best friend later tells him that many children in Japan are dying of hunger, a painful reminder of the real world.

Siberia cakes were popular in Japan from the 1920s through the 1960s. Made of a sort of sponge cake called *kasutera* (or *castella*), the treats are filled with a layer of red bean paste. These nostalgic cakes enjoyed renewed popularity after the film was released.

INGREDIENTS

½ cup unsalted butter

½ cup whole milk

7 eggs

¾ cup plus 2 tablespoons (115 grams) flour

½ cup plus 2 tablespoons (115 grams) sugar

½ cup water

18 ounces red bean paste

0.35 ounces (10 grams) agar-agar powder

DIFFICULTY:

YIELD: 8 servings

TIME: 1 hour, 30 minutes
(+4 hours in refrigerator)

DIRECTIONS

1 Warm the butter with the milk in a saucepan over medium heat, stirring frequently. When the butter is thoroughly melted, remove it from the heat and let cool.

2 Separate the egg yolks and whites into two different bowls. Sift the flour into a mixing bowl and incorporate the warm milk mixture to form a batter. Add the egg yolks one-third at a time, mixing between each addition.

3 Whisk the egg whites as you slowly pour in the sugar to produce a light, runny meringue that sticks to the whisk.

4 Gradually add the meringue to the batter until it is completely consistent in color.

5 Preheat the oven to 300°F. Pour the batter into a large rectangular pan lined with parchment paper. Place the cake pan into a broiler pan with about an inch of water in the bottom. Bake at 300°F for 1 hour; then take the cake pan out of the broiler pan and let it cool for 10 minutes before removing the cake from its pan.

6 While the cake is cooling, boil the ½ cup of water, add the red bean paste and agar-agar powder, and warm until the ingredients have fully dissolved. Let cool.

7 Cut the cake in half. Spread the red bean paste evenly over the surface of one half. Lay the other half over the top, leaving the more browned side exposed. Refrigerate for 4 hours.

8 Cut the cake into triangles before serving.

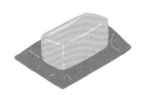 

ITADAKIMASU!

PINEAPPLE UPSIDE-DOWN CAKE

BACKGROUND

Only Yesterday strings together scenes from Taeko's childhood in the city, when she dreamed of escaping to the country. The flashbacks allow us to see Japanese society in 1966 through the eyes of a ten-year-old girl. The 1960s were a time of rapid economic development and internationalization for Japan, and Taeko's wavering between city and country life mirrors Japan's own wavering between its traditional past and its modern incarnation.

One day, Taeko convinces her father to buy a whole pineapple in the luxury district of Ginza. However, her city-dwelling family has no idea how to eat it! After all, most Japanese people have only ever encountered this exotic fruit in a can. The family members spend several days figuring out how to prepare the pineapple, but they are ultimately disappointed to find that it doesn't taste very sweet.

There's something comical in the way the entire family crowds around the mother as she peels and cuts up the pineapple, watching the fruit as they might observe a strange animal. This recipe for a pineapple upside-down cake surely would have impressed Taeko and her family.

INGREDIENTS

For the cake:

6 tablespoons (80 grams) unsalted butter, softened

1 cup plus 1 tablespoon (230 grams) sugar, divided

1 tablespoon vanilla extract

3 eggs

1½ cups (180 grams) flour

2 teaspoons baking powder

Pinch of salt

Splash of rum (optional)

For the caramel:

4 tablespoons water

Dash of lemon juice (optional)

1 can pineapple slices

DIFFICULTY: ❀ ❀ ❀ • •

YIELD: 4 servings

TIME: 1 hour

DIRECTIONS

1 Cream the butter, 6 tablespoons of sugar, and vanilla in a bowl.

2 In a separate bowl, beat the eggs, add them into the butter mixture, and stir to combine.

3 Slowly sift the flour and baking powder into the mixture while stirring. Add the pinch of salt and the rum, if desired, and beat again..

4 Thoroughly grease a cake pan, and then line the bottom with a piece of aluminum foil cut to match the shape. Flatten out the foil, and grease it as well. Preheat the oven to 350°F.

5 **Prepare the caramel:** Dissolve the remaining sugar with the water in a saucepan over low heat, and mix thoroughly. Add the lemon, if desired. When the mixture begins to brown, stir it in large, circular movements.

6 Pour the caramel into the cake pan, making sure to cover the entire surface.

7 Arrange the pineapple slices atop the caramel. Pour the batter over the top, and smooth the surface.

8 Bake for 45 minutes at 350°F. Turn the cake out upside down, and let it cool slightly before serving.

ITADAKIMASU!

CHOCOLATE CAKE

BACKGROUND

In *Kiki's Delivery Service*, Kiki goes to much effort to deliver an unwanted herring and pumpkin pie. Afterward, Madame asks her to make another delivery. This second parcel turns out to be a delicious-looking chocolate cake with glossy icing, decorated meticulously with Kiki's name and an image of her on her broomstick.

Madame asks Kiki to find out the recipient's birthday while she's at it so that she can bake her another cake. Kiki jokes in return that the recipient will probably want to know Madame's birthday, too, so that she can think of a suitable present.

This discussion of birthdays refers back to the delivery of the unappreciated homemade pie. The scene implies that the two women have become friends: Kiki needs someone to care about her in this city, and Madame has love to give. The chocolate cake is not only a treat for the tastebuds, but also a balm for the heart.

INGREDIENTS

For the cake:

4 eggs

1½ cups plus 2 tablespoons (320 grams) sugar, divided

¼ cup milk

½ teaspoon vanilla extract

¼ cup (35 grams) flour

¾ cup plus 2 tablespoons (100 grams) cocoa powder, divided

2 teaspoons baking powder

For the icing:

½ cup water

½ cup cream

5 or 6 gelatin sheets

Fondant in white, green, and red (optional)

DIFFICULTY: 🕷🕷🕷🕷 •

YIELD: 6 servings

TIME: 1 hour, 45 minutes

DIRECTIONS

1 Separate the egg yolks and whites into two different mixing bowls. Beat the yolks, then add 4 tablespoons (50 grams) of sugar. Stir until smooth.

2 Pour in the milk and vanilla, and sift in the flour, ⅓ cup of cocoa powder, and the baking powder. Stir well.

3 Beat the egg whites until frothy, then pour in another 4 tablespoons (50 grams) of sugar, one-third at a time. Stop beating before the egg whites become too firm; they should be slightly runny.

4 Fold the egg whites into the batter. Pour the batter into a greased or lined round cake pan. Preheat the oven to 250°F.

5 Place the cake pan into a larger dish containing hot water to create a double boiler. Place the entire dish in the oven, and bakeat 250°F for 20 minutes, 300°F for 20 minutes, 230°F for 30 minutes, and then 350°F for 5 minutes. Remove and let cool.

6 In a saucepan, boil the water with the remaining sugar. When the liquid turns opaque, remove it from the heat.

7 Add the remaining cocoa powder and the cream. Whisk together and return the saucepan to the heat.

8 Place the gelatin sheets in a container with cool water for 1 minute. When the gelatin sheets have softened, add them to the saucepan and stir.

9 When the icing is smooth and even, strain and let cool.

10 Remove the cake from the pan, and place it on a wire rack. Pour the icing in an even layer over the cake. Set aside.

11 *Optional*: Knead the fondant to form slightly soft balls, then roll them out with a rolling pin.

12 *Optional:* On a sheet of paper, draw Kiki the witch, Jiji the cat, a small pine tree, and the letters *K I K I*, as shown. Cut the fondant to match the shapes, and arrange the fondant decorations on the cake.

ITADAKIMASU!

INSIGHT
EDITIONS

PO Box 3088
San Rafael, CA 94912
www.insighteditions.com

Find us on Facebook: www.facebook.com/InsightEditions
Follow us on Instagram: @insighteditions

ISBN: 978-1-64722-912-2

Publisher: Raoul Goff
VP of Licensing and Partnerships: Vanessa Lopez
VP of Manufacturing: Alix Nicholaeff
VP, Editorial Director: Vicki Jaeger
Senior Designer: Monique Narboneta Zosa
Editor: Anna Wostenberg
Editorial Assistant: Grace Orriss
Senior Production Editor: Katie Rokakis
Production Associate: Deena Hashem
Senior Production Manager, Subsidiary Rights:
    Lina s Palma-Temena

C/O YNNIS ÉDITIONS
38 Rue Notre-Dame-de-Nazareth
75003 PARIS
www.ynnis-editions.fr
Ynnis Éditions
@YnnisEditions

Recipes by Minh-Tri Vo
Photography concocted by Apolline Cartier
Texts cooked up by Claire-France Thévenon

Top-shelf publication management by Cedric Littardi
Editorial direction deglazed by Sébastien Rost
French publication braised by Philippe Vallotti
Proofreading tenderized by Eugénie Michel
Cover finely diced by Sébastien Rost
Layout and original illustrations staged by Cerise Heurteur
Printing marinated by Céline Antoine
Communication and marketing flambéed by
Camille Nogueira, Thomas Thus
Coordination cooked to taste by Jeanne Bucher
This book is in no way an official Ghibli publication.
It is a cookbook featuring real recipes for food
that appears in the studio's films

Originally published in France by Ynnis Editions in 2020
under the title "La Cuisine des Films du Studio Ghibli".

ROOTS of PEACE   REPLANTED PAPER

Insight Editions, in association with Roots of Peace,
will plant two trees for each tree used in the manufacturing
of this book. Roots of Peace is an internationally renowned
humanitarian organization dedicated to eradicating land
mines worldwide and converting war-torn lands into
 productive farms and wildlife habitats. Roots of Peace
will plant two million fruit and nut trees in Afghanistan
and provide farmers there with the skills and support
necessary for sustainable land use.

Manufactured in China by Insight Editions

10 9 8 7 6 5